cor

MW01103506

British & North American Readers:
Please note that Australian cup and
spoon measurements are metric. A quick
conversion guide appears on page 63.
A glossary explaining unfamiliar terms
and ingredients begins on page 60.

2 no-fat salad dressings

These dressings are perfect – they lend the piquancy necessary to make a salad truly special without doing dastardly things to your waistline.

soy and ginger dressing

1/4 cup (60ml) rice vinegar

2 tablespoons light soy sauce

1 tablespoon lemon juice

2 teaspoons sugar

1/2 teaspoon grated fresh ginger

Combine ingredients in screw-top jar; shake well.

MAKES 1/2 cup (125ml)
Per tablespoon
0g fat; 65kJ

sweet chilli dressing

1/4 cup (60ml) rice vinegar

2 tablespoons sweet chilli sauce

1 teaspoon fish sauce

1 teaspoon finely chopped fresh coriander

Combine ingredients in screw-top jar; shake well.

MAKES 1/3 cup (80ml)
Per tablespoon 0g fat; 60kJ

mustard and honey dressing

1 tablespoon honey

1/4 cup (60ml) orange juice

2 teaspoons seeded mustard

1 teaspoon finely chopped fresh thyme

Combine ingredients in screw-top jar; shake well.

MAKES 1/3 cup (80ml)
Per tablespoon 0g fat; 130kJ

garlic balsamic dressing

1 medium bulb garlic (70g)

1 tablespoon balsamic vinegar

¼ cup (60ml) white wine vinegar

2 teaspoons sugar

Tightly wrap whole garlic bulb in piece of foil; roast in moderate oven about 50 minutes or until garlic is soft, cool 15 minutes. **Squeeze** garlic pulp from cloves; blend or process with remaining ingredients until smooth.

MAKES ⅓ cup (80ml)
Per tablespoon 0g fat; 113kJ

from left to right: sweet chilli dressing; soy and ginger dressing; garlic balsamic dressing; mustard and honey dressing

char-grilled salmon

and limes with creamy herb sauce

4 small salmon
fillets (600g)

1/4 cup (85g) lime
marmalade

1 tablespoon
rice vinegar

1 teaspoon grated
fresh ginger

3 medium limes
(240g), sliced thickly

creamy herb sauce

1/2 cup (140g)
low-fat yogurt

2 teaspoons finely
chopped fresh mint

1 teaspoon finely
chopped fresh dill

Brush salmon with combined marmalade, vinegar and ginger.
Cook salmon and lime slices on heated oiled grill plate (or grill or barbecue) until salmon is browned both sides and cooked as desired and lime slices are browned both sides.
Serve salmon and lime with creamy herb sauce.
Creamy Herb Sauce Combine ingredients in small bowl.

SERVES 4
Per serving 11.4g fat; 1267kJ

6 tomato

and borlotti bean soup

2 medium brown onions (300g), chopped coarsely

2 cloves garlic, crushed

11 large egg tomatoes (1kg), chopped coarsely

2 cups (500ml) chicken stock

1 tablespoon worcestershire sauce

2 tablespoons finely chopped fresh flat-leaf parsley

2 x 400g cans borlotti beans, rinsed, drained

Heat oiled large saucepan; cook onion and garlic, stirring, until onion softens. Stir in tomato; cook, stirring, about 3 minutes or until tomato softens. Add stock and sauce, bring to a boil; simmer, covered, 15 minutes.

Blend or process tomato mixture, in batches, until almost smooth. Return tomato mixture to pan, stir in parsley and beans; simmer, uncovered, about 5 minutes or until hot.

SERVES 4
Per serving 0.8g fat; 417kJ

char-grilled chicken
with mango salsa

4 single chicken breast fillets (700g)

120g spinach, shredded finely

1 medium red onion (170g), chopped finely

1 medium mango (430g), chopped finely

1 tablespoon coarsely chopped fresh mint

1/4 cup (20g) flaked parmesan cheese

1/4 cup (60ml) sweet chilli sauce

Cook chicken on heated oiled grill plate (or grill or barbecue) until browned both sides and cooked through.
Meanwhile, combine spinach, onion, mango, mint, cheese and sauce in medium bowl; mix well.
Serve chicken topped with salsa.

SERVES 4
Per serving
6.3g fat; 1222kJ

teriyaki beef skewers

2 large red onions (600g)

500g beef rump steak, sliced thinly

1/4 cup (60ml) teriyaki sauce

1 tablespoon tomato paste

1 clove garlic, crushed

1 teaspoon brown sugar

2 green onions, sliced thinly

Cut red onions in half; cut each half into six wedges. Thread onion wedges and beef onto 12 skewers.

Combine sauce, paste, garlic and sugar in small bowl, brush sauce mixture over skewers, cover; refrigerate 3 hours or until required.

Cook beef skewers on heated oiled grill plate (or grill or barbecue) until browned all over and cooked as desired.

Serve beef skewers sprinkled with green onion.

SERVES 4
Per serving 8.6g fat; 1042kJ

light **caesar** salad

4 thick slices bread

2 bacon rashers

4 anchovy fillets, drained

1 large cos lettuce

⅓ cup (25g) flaked parmesan cheese

light caesar dressing

½ cup (100g) low-fat cottage cheese

½ teaspoon dijon mustard

1 tablespoon lemon juice

¼ cup (60ml) skim milk

Remove and discard crusts from bread; cut bread into 1.5cm cubes. Place bread cubes in single layer on oven tray; bake, uncovered, in moderate oven about 10 minutes or until browned lightly.

Trim any fat from bacon; chop bacon coarsely. Cook bacon in small non-stick frying pan, stirring, until crisp; drain on absorbent paper.

Rinse oil from anchovies; pat dry on absorbent paper. Reserve half of the anchovies for light caesar dressing; chop the remainder.

Arrange torn lettuce leaves, bacon and half of the croutons in large bowl; toss gently. Serve salad sprinkled with the remaining croutons, cheese, remaining anchovies and drizzled with light caesar dressing.

Light Caesar Dressing Blend or process the reserved anchovies with remaining ingredients until smooth.

SERVES 4
Per serving 6.6g fat; 963kJ

gingered pork
with stir-fried vegetables

Combine sauce, wine, golden syrup, sugar, garlic and ginger in large bowl, add pork; mix well. Cover; refrigerate 3 hours or until required.
Preheat oven to moderate. Drain pork over small bowl; reserve marinade. Cook pork in heated large non-stick frying pan until browned all over. Transfer pork to wire rack over baking dish; bake pork, uncovered, in moderate oven about 30 minutes or until cooked through. Cool 5 minutes; slice thinly.
Heat oil in wok or large frying pan; stir-fry onion, carrot and zucchini, tossing, until vegetables are just tender. Blend cornflour with reserved marinade and enough water to make 1 cup (250ml) liquid. Add to pan with snow peas and sprouts, stir until sauce boils and thickens slightly.
Serve pork with stir-fried vegetables.

SERVES 4
Per serving 3.3g fat; 830kJ

1/4 cup (60ml)
light soy sauce

2 tablespoons dry
red wine

1 tablespoon
golden syrup

1 tablespoon
brown sugar

2 cloves garlic,
crushed

1 tablespoon
grated fresh ginger

2 pork fillets (500g)

2 teaspoons
peanut oil

1 medium brown
onion (150g),
chopped coarsely

1 small carrot
(70g), sliced thinly

1 medium
zucchini (120g),
sliced thinly

2 teaspoons
cornflour

150g snow peas,
halved

1 1/4 cups (100g)
bean sprouts

roast pork
with rosemary

1 teaspoon
olive oil

2 cloves garlic,
crushed

1 tablespoon
finely chopped
fresh rosemary

1 large brown
onion (200g),
chopped finely

150g button
mushrooms,
sliced thinly

500g spinach,
chopped coarsely

3 pork fillets (750g)

sauce

1 teaspoon
cornflour

1/2 cup (125ml)
chicken stock

1/2 teaspoon
balsamic vinegar

1/2 teaspoon
finely chopped
fresh rosemary

Heat oil in large non-stick frying pan; cook garlic, rosemary, onion and mushrooms, stirring, until onion is soft. Add spinach; cook, stirring, until spinach is just wilted, cool.

Preheat oven to moderately hot. Cut a pocket in each fillet, fill with spinach mixture; secure with kitchen string. Cook pork fillets in heated oiled large frying pan until browned all over. Place pork on wire rack in baking dish; bake pork, uncovered, in moderately hot oven about 30 minutes or until cooked through. Cover pork to keep warm; reserve any pan juices. Serve pork with sauce.

Sauce Blend cornflour with reserved pan juices and remaining ingredients in small saucepan; stir over heat until sauce boils and thickens slightly.

SERVES 4
Per serving 6g fat; 1075kJ

deep-dish eggplant
and pasta torte

3 large eggplants (1.5kg)

coarse cooking salt

cooking-oil spray

375g penne

1 cup (250ml) tomato pasta sauce

2 tablespoons tomato paste

1 cup (100g) coarsely grated low-fat mozzarella cheese

1/2 cup (40g) finely grated parmesan cheese

1 tablespoon finely chopped fresh basil

2 eggs, beaten lightly

1 tablespoon packaged breadcrumbs

Lightly oil deep 23cm round cake pan. Cut eggplants into 3mm slices, place slices in colander; sprinkle with salt, stand 30 minutes. Rinse eggplant under cold water; drain on absorbent paper. Coat eggplant slices with cooking-oil spray; grill until browned both sides and tender.

Preheat oven to moderate.

Cook pasta in large saucepan of boiling water, uncovered, until just tender; drain.

Combine pasta with sauce, paste, cheeses, basil and egg in large bowl.

Place a large eggplant slice in centre of prepared pan, reserve about ten slices of eggplant for top; place remaining eggplant slices around centre slice to cover base and side of pan. Spoon pasta mixture into pan, arrange reserved eggplant slices over top; sprinkle with breadcrumbs.

Bake, uncovered, in moderate oven about 30 minutes or until firm. Stand 10 minutes before serving.

SERVES 6
Per serving 9.7g fat; 1653kJ

swordfish

with beans and tomatoes

12 medium egg
tomatoes (900g),
halved

2 teaspoons olive oil

1 tablespoon
brown sugar

2 tablespoons
balsamic vinegar

2 cloves garlic,
crushed

1 teaspoon salt

1/2 teaspoon cracked
black pepper

350g baby green
beans, trimmed

4 (800g) swordfish
fillets

10 fresh basil
leaves, torn

Preheat oven to hot. Combine tomato, oil, sugar, vinegar, garlic,
salt and pepper in large baking dish. Roast, uncovered, in hot oven
about 35 minutes or until tomato is soft.
Meanwhile, boil, steam or microwave beans until tender. Cook fish
on heated oiled grill plate (or grill or barbecue) until browned both
sides and just cooked through. Stir basil into tomato mixture;
serve with fish and beans.

SERVES 4
Per serving 7.1g fat; 1217kJ

thai beef salad

500g beef rump steak

¼ cup (60ml) lime juice

2 tablespoons finely shredded fresh mint

150g spinach

2 lebanese cucumbers (260g), seeded, sliced thinly

1 tablespoon white wine vinegar

2 tablespoons fish sauce

1 tablespoon brown sugar

Combine beef with juice and mint in medium bowl, cover; refrigerate at least 3 hours or until required.
Heat oiled large frying pan; cook beef until browned both sides and cooked as desired. Cover beef, rest 5 minutes; cut into thin slices. Combine beef with spinach and cucumber in large bowl.
Gently toss combined vinegar, sauce and sugar through beef salad.

SERVES 4
Per serving 8.6g fat; 954kJ

spicy **tofu** salad

750g firm tofu, drained

1 small red
onion (100g)

1 medium carrot (120g)

1 medium green
capsicum (200g)

2 tablespoons
coarsely chopped
unsalted roasted
peanuts

dressing

2 red thai chillies,
chopped finely

1/4 cup (60ml)
lime juice

2 tablespoons
brown sugar

1 tablespoon
fish sauce

1 stem fresh lemon
grass, sliced thinly

Cut tofu into 1cm cubes. Cut onion in half; then cut into thin slices.
Cut carrot and capsicum into thin strips.
Combine tofu, onion, carrot, capsicum and dressing in large bowl,
cover; refrigerate 3 hours. Serve salad sprinkled with nuts.
Dressing Combine ingredients in screw-top jar; shake well.

SERVES 4
Per serving 12.3g fat; 1211kJ

beef and leeks with
crispy rice noodles

500g beef steak,
sliced thinly

$1/2$ teaspoon
sesame oil

4cm piece fresh
ginger, sliced thinly

2 tablespoons
dry sherry

1 tablespoon
soy sauce

80g rice vermicelli
noodles

vegetable oil,
for deep-frying

1 tablespoon
vegetable oil, extra

2 medium leeks
(700g), sliced thinly

2 medium carrots
(240g), sliced thinly

2 trimmed sticks
celery (150g),
sliced thinly

2 teaspoons
cornflour

1 cup (250ml)
beef stock

Combine beef, sesame oil, ginger, sherry and sauce
in medium bowl, cover; refrigerate at least 3 hours.
Break noodles into pieces; deep-fry in hot vegetable
oil until puffed, drain on absorbent paper.
Heat extra vegetable oil in wok or large frying
pan; stir-fry beef mixture, in batches, until beef
is browned. Stir-fry leek. Add carrot and celery;
stir-fry. Return beef to wok with blended cornflour
and stock; stir until mixture boils and thickens
slightly. Serve stir-fry with noodles.

SERVES 4
Per serving 12.6g fat; 1308kJ

tandoori

chicken salad

500g chicken tenderloins, halved lengthways

2 tablespoons tandoori paste

1 cos lettuce

1 medium mango (430g), sliced thinly

2 trimmed celery sticks (150g), sliced thinly

1 lebanese cucumber (130g), seeded, sliced thinly

1 small red onion (100g), sliced thinly

2 tablespoons small fresh mint leaves

2 tablespoons unsalted roasted peanuts

yogurt mint dressing

1/2 cup (140g) low-fat yogurt

2 tablespoons water

1/2 teaspoon tandoori paste

pinch ground cumin

1 small clove garlic, crushed

1 tablespoon finely chopped fresh mint

Combine chicken and paste in medium bowl. Cook chicken in heated oiled large non-stick frying pan until browned all over and cooked through.
Combine torn lettuce leaves in large bowl with mango, celery, cucumber and onion, top with chicken; drizzle with dressing.
Serve sprinkled with mint leaves and nuts.
Yogurt Mint Dressing Whisk ingredients in small bowl until combined.

SERVES 4
Per serving
13.2g fat; 1420kJ

chicken with
green beans and noodles

150g bean thread vermicelli noodles

2 teaspoons peanut oil

500g chicken thigh fillets, halved

250g green beans

2 cloves garlic, crushed

1 medium brown onion (150g), sliced thinly

2 tablespoons fish sauce

2 tablespoons light soy sauce

2 teaspoons lime juice

1 tablespoon cornflour

1 tablespoon water

2 tablespoons finely chopped fresh basil

Place noodles in large heatproof bowl, cover with boiling water; stand 5 minutes, drain.
Heat half of the oil in wok or large frying pan; stir-fry chicken, in batches, until browned all over and cooked through, drain on absorbent paper.
Boil, steam or microwave beans until just tender. Rinse beans under cold water; drain.
Add remaining oil to pan; stir-fry garlic and onion until onion is just soft. Return chicken to pan with noodles, beans, sauces, juice and blended cornflour and water; stir over heat until mixture boils and thickens. Stir in basil.

SERVES 4
Per serving 12g fat; 1464kJ

asian-glazed swordfish
with baby bok choy

4 (800g) swordfish fillets

1 tablespoon hoisin sauce

2 tablespoons light soy sauce

1 tablespoon sweet chilli sauce

1 clove garlic, crushed

1/2 teaspoon sesame oil

2 tablespoons rice vinegar

1 teaspoon sugar

600g baby bok choy, halved lengthways

1/4 cup loosely packed fresh coriander leaves

Coat fish fillets with half the combined sauces, garlic and oil. Add vinegar and sugar to remaining sauce mixture; reserve dressing.

Cook fish fillets in heated oiled large non-stick frying pan until browned both sides and just cooked through. Remove fish from pan, cover to keep warm.

Add bok choy to same pan; cook, covered, until just tender. Serve fish on bok choy, drizzled with reserved dressing; sprinkle with coriander.

SERVES 4
Per serving 5.7g fat; 1055kJ

glazed racks of lamb
with beans and asparagus

*4 (780g) trimmed
racks of lamb
(3 cutlets in each)*

*2 tablespoons
orange marmalade*

2 tablespoons honey

*2 teaspoons
seeded mustard*

1 teaspoon olive oil

1 clove garlic, crushed

*250g green
beans, halved*

*250g asparagus,
halved*

Preheat oven to hot. Place racks of lamb on wire rack over baking dish, brush with half of the combined marmalade, honey and mustard. Pour 2 cups (500ml) boiling water into baking dish. Roast lamb, uncovered, in hot oven about 20 minutes or until cooked as desired. Cover lamb, rest 5 minutes.

Meanwhile, heat oil in wok or large frying pan; stir-fry garlic, beans and asparagus, tossing, until vegetables are just tender. Add remaining marmalade mixture, tossing, until vegetables are glazed. Serve lamb with glazed vegetables.

SERVES 4
Per serving 10.4g fat; 1173kJ

chicken and vegetable
soup with parmesan bread

500g chicken
thigh fillets,
chopped coarsely

1 small leek (200g),
chopped finely

2 medium carrots
(240g), chopped finely

1 medium potato
(200g), chopped finely

400g can tomatoes

2 cups (500ml)
chicken stock

1 litre (4 cups) water

2 medium zucchini
(240g), chopped finely

300g can butter
beans, rinsed, drained

2 teaspoons
finely chopped
fresh oregano

1 small french
breadstick

cooking-oil spray

2 tablespoons
finely grated
parmesan cheese

Place chicken, leek, carrot, potato, undrained
crushed tomatoes, stock and the water in large
saucepan, bring to boil; simmer, covered, 1 hour.
Add zucchini, beans and oregano; simmer,
covered, about 15 minutes or until zucchini
is tender.
Meanwhile, cut breadstick into 2cm thick
diagonal slices; coat one side of each slice
with cooking-oil spray, sprinkle with cheese;
grill until cheese is browned lightly.
Serve soup with parmesan bread.

SERVES 4
Per serving 12.4g fat; 1632kJ

prawn and couscous salad
with lemon dressing

1 cup (200g) couscous

1 cup (250ml)
boiling water

500g medium
cooked prawns

1 lebanese cucumber
(130g), sliced thinly

1 medium red
capsicum (200g),
chopped finely

1 cup loosely packed
fresh coriander

1 cup tightly packed
watercress

lemon dressing

1 teaspoon finely
grated lemon rind

1/3 cup (80ml)
lemon juice

2 cloves garlic,
crushed

2 tablespoons
fish sauce

2 tablespoons
finely chopped
fresh coriander

Place couscous in medium heatproof bowl,
add the boiling water; stand 5 minutes, fluff
couscous with a fork to separate grains.
Shell and devein prawns, leaving tails intact.
Combine couscous, prawns, cucumber,
capsicum, coriander and watercress in
large bowl. Just before serving, add lemon
dressing; toss gently.
Lemon Dressing Combine ingredients in
screw-top jar; shake well.

SERVES 4
Per serving 1g fat; 1128kJ

black and white
sesame-crusted lamb

2 cloves garlic, crushed

1 tablespoon lemon juice

1 tablespoon finely chopped fresh flat-leaf parsley

2 teaspoons dijon mustard

500g lamb eye of loin

1 tablespoon white sesame seeds

1 tablespoon black sesame seeds

Preheat oven to very hot. Combine garlic, juice, parsley and mustard in small bowl. Place lamb on wire rack over baking dish; brush garlic mixture all over lamb, sprinkle with combined seeds.

Bake lamb, uncovered, in very hot oven about 15 minutes or until lamb is browned all over and cooked as desired. Cover lamb, rest 5 minutes; cut into slices just before serving.

SERVES 4
Per serving 8.3g fat; 813kJ

onion, spinach and cheese frittata

1 teaspoon olive oil

3 medium brown onions (450g), sliced thinly

2 cloves garlic, crushed

100g spinach leaves, shredded finely

4 eggs, beaten lightly

60g low-fat cheddar cheese, chopped finely

1/3 cup (65g) low-fat ricotta cheese

1 tablespoon finely grated parmesan cheese

1 tablespoon finely shredded fresh basil

1 tablespoon finely chopped fresh sage

Heat oil in medium saucepan; cook onion and garlic, covered, stirring occasionally, 20 minutes or until onion is very soft. Add spinach; stir until wilted. Combine onion mixture with eggs, cheeses and herbs in medium bowl; mix well. Pour egg mixture into heated oiled 24cm non-stick frying pan; cook over low heat about 10 minutes or until centre begins to set. **Place** under grill; grill until frittata is set and top is browned lightly.

SERVES 4
Per serving 9.7g fat; 768kJ

spiced lamb and vegetables
with COUSCOUS

1 medium eggplant
(300g), chopped
coarsely

2 medium zucchini
(240g), chopped
coarsely

1 medium brown onion
(150g), sliced thinly

1 clove garlic, crushed

1/2 teaspoon
ground cinnamon

1 teaspoon
ground turmeric

2 teaspoons
ground cumin

1/2 teaspoon
ground ginger

1 tablespoon plain flour

2 cups (500ml)
beef stock

1 tablespoon
lemon juice

1 tablespoon pine
nuts, toasted

2 tablespoons chopped
fresh coriander

8 lamb cutlets (500g)

3/4 cup (180ml)
boiling water

3/4 cup (150g) couscous

Cook eggplant, zucchini and onion in heated
large non-stick saucepan, stirring, until
vegetables soften. Add garlic, spices and
flour; cook, stirring, until fragrant.
Gradually stir in stock, juice and nuts; stir until
mixture boils and thickens. Stir in coriander.
Grill cutlets until browned both sides and
cooked as desired.
Meanwhile, place the water in medium
heatproof bowl, add couscous; stand,
covered, 5 minutes or until water is
absorbed. Fluff couscous with fork.
Serve couscous with lamb and vegetables.

SERVES 4
Per serving 9.4g fat; 1356kJ

vegetarian
lasagne

3 medium red capsicums (600g)

4 medium zucchini (480g)

4 baby eggplants (240g)

cooking-oil spray

1 teaspoon olive oil

1 medium brown onion (150g), chopped finely

2 cloves garlic, crushed

600ml tomato pasta sauce with basil

1 tablespoon finely chopped fresh basil

6 large instant lasagne sheets

1¼ cups (250g) low-fat ricotta cheese

½ cup (60g) coarsely grated low-fat cheddar

¼ cup (20g) finely grated parmesan

Quarter capsicums, remove and discard seeds and membranes. Roast under grill or in very hot oven, skin-side up, until skin blisters and blackens. Cover capsicum pieces with plastic or paper for 5 minutes; peel away skin and discard.

Cut zucchini and eggplants lengthways into 5mm thick slices, coat with cooking-oil spray; grill until browned both sides and tender.

Preheat oven to moderate. Heat oil in large frying pan; cook onion and garlic, stirring, until onion is soft. Add pasta sauce and fresh basil.

Place two lasagne sheets into 6cm-deep, 2-litre (8 cup) rectangular ovenproof dish. Top with capsicum and a quarter of the tomato sauce. Continue layering with two sheets of pasta, eggplant and a quarter of the tomato sauce, then remaining pasta and zucchini; spread over ricotta. Spoon over remaining tomato sauce; sprinkle with combined cheddar and parmesan.

Bake, uncovered, in moderate oven about 1 hour or until top is browned and pasta is tender.

SERVES 4
Per serving 12.4g fat; 1659kJ

spicy beef
soup

375g beef round steak, sliced thinly

1 tablespoon dry red wine

3 cups (750ml) water

3 cups (750ml) beef stock

6 green onions, chopped finely

2 cloves garlic, sliced thinly

3 fresh coriander roots

2 tablespoons light soy sauce

2 teaspoons brown sugar

1 red thai chilli, chopped finely

425g can straw mushrooms, drained

1/4 cup (60ml) lime juice

1 tablespoon finely chopped fresh coriander leaves

Combine beef and wine in medium bowl, cover; stand 15 minutes.

Combine the water, beef stock, onion, garlic, coriander roots, sauce, sugar and half of the chilli in large saucepan. Bring to a boil; simmer, uncovered, 15 minutes. Strain soup, return strained stock to saucepan; discard onion mixture.

Just before serving, bring stock to a boil; add beef, mushrooms, remaining chilli and juice; simmer, uncovered, until hot. Stir in coriander leaves.

SERVES 4
Per serving 5.3g fat; 650kJ

hot-sour chicken

and snake beans

4 cloves garlic,
crushed

1 teaspoon cracked
black pepper

2 teaspoons finely
grated lemon rind

4 red thai
chillies, seeded,
chopped finely

1/2 cup (125ml) water

2 tablespoons thick
tamarind concentrate

1kg chicken breast
fillets, sliced thinly

350g snake beans,
chopped coarsely

2 large red onions
(600g), sliced thinly

1 tablespoon sugar

1/4 cup (60ml)
chicken stock

Combine garlic, pepper, rind, chilli, the water,
tamarind and chicken in medium bowl, cover;
refrigerate at least 3 hours or until required.
Boil, steam or microwave beans until just
tender; drain.
Cook chicken mixture and onion in heated
large non-stick frying pan, in batches, until
chicken and onion are cooked through. Return
chicken to pan with beans, sugar and stock;
cook, tossing, until sauce boils.

SERVES 6
Per serving 9.6g fat; 1206kJ

32 light & easy side serves

*The tasty dishes featured in this book are all the more tantalising when
served with one (or more!) of the following accompaniments.*

garlic roasted baby potatoes

1kg baby new potatoes

1 teaspoon olive oil

1 teaspoon sichuan pepper

18 unpeeled cloves garlic

6 sprigs fresh thyme

Preheat oven to moderately hot.
Combine ingredients in baking
dish; mix well. Roast, uncovered,
in moderately hot oven about
45 minutes or until potatoes
are browned and tender, stirring
twice during cooking.

SERVES 6
Per serving 1g fat; 475kJ

green beans with tomatoes and oregano

400g green beans, halved

*3 large egg tomatoes (270g),
seeded, chopped finely*

*½ small red onion (50g),
chopped finely*

1 teaspoon olive oil

*1 teaspoon finely chopped
fresh oregano*

Boil, steam or microwave beans until
tender; drain. Combine remaining
ingredients in small bowl. Spoon
tomato mixture over hot beans.

SERVES 4
Per serving 1.4g fat; 184kJ

asian stir-fried vegies

2 cloves garlic, crushed

1 teaspoon grated fresh ginger

½ teaspoon sesame oil

250g choy sum, chopped coarsely

*250g baby bok choy,
chopped coarsely*

2 tablespoons hoisin sauce

Heat oiled wok or large frying
pan; cook garlic and ginger,
stirring, until fragrant.
Add remaining ingredients;
stir-fry until vegetables are
just wilted.

SERVES 4
Per serving 1.5g fat; 178kJ

green salad with citrus dressing

100g snow peas

50g snow pea sprouts

150g mesclun

1 small clove garlic, crushed

1 teaspoon olive oil

1 tablespoon white wine vinegar

1 tablespoon lemon juice

2 tablespoons orange juice

Cut snow peas into very thin strips.
Combine peas, sprouts and
mesclun in large bowl. Combine
remaining ingredients in screw-top
jar; shake well. Gently toss salad
with dressing.

SERVES 4
Per serving 1.4g fat; 193kJ

veal with tomato
olive sauce

2 teaspoons olive oil

4 veal steaks (600g)

1 medium brown onion (150g), sliced thinly

1 clove garlic, crushed

1 tablespoon finely chopped fresh oregano

1/3 cup (80ml) water

2 teaspoons red wine vinegar

2 tablespoons tomato paste

400g can tomatoes

1/2 cup (80g) seeded black olives

1 tablespoon drained capers

1 tablespoon finely chopped fresh flat-leaf parsley

Heat oil in large non-stick frying pan; cook veal until browned both sides, remove veal from pan. **Cook** onion, garlic, oregano and the water in same pan, stirring, until onion softens. Add vinegar, paste and undrained crushed tomatoes; simmer, uncovered, about 10 minutes or until sauce thickens slightly. **Return** veal to pan with olives; simmer, uncovered, until veal is just heated through. **Serve** the veal and tomato olive sauce sprinkled with capers and parsley.

SERVES 4
Per serving 7.9g fat; 1610kJ

warm mushroom

and capsicum pasta salad

1 medium red
capsicum (200g)

1 medium green
capsicum (200g)

250g button mushrooms,
sliced thinly

1 small red onion (100g),
sliced thinly

1/4 cup (60ml) water

250g rigatoni pasta

1/2 cup (125ml) oil-free
italian dressing

2 tablespoons finely
chopped fresh
flat-leaf parsley

2 tablespoons finely
grated parmesan cheese

Quarter capsicums, remove and discard seeds and membranes.
Roast under grill or in very hot oven, skin-side up, until skin blisters
and blackens. Cover capsicum pieces with plastic or paper for
5 minutes; peel away skin and discard. Cut capsicum into thin slices.
Combine mushrooms, onion and the water in large frying pan;
cook, stirring, until mushrooms soften. Add capsicum; stir until hot.
Cook pasta in large saucepan of boiling water, uncovered, until
just tender; drain. Toss pasta with vegetable mixture, dressing
and parsley. Serve sprinkled with cheese.

SERVES 4
Per serving 2.2g fat; 1229kJ

*500g chicken
breast fillets*

*2 tablespoons
kecap manis*

*250g asparagus,
chopped coarsely*

*1 medium
carrot (120g)*

100g snow peas

100g bean sprouts

*100g snow pea
sprouts*

*2 cups (160g) finely
shredded cabbage*

*2 green onions,
chopped finely*

*2 tablespoons slivered
almonds, toasted*

*1 tablespoon
white sesame
seeds, toasted*

dressing

*2 tablespoons
light soy sauce*

*2 tablespoons
rice vinegar*

*1/2 teaspoon grated
fresh ginger*

1/4 teaspoon wasabi

Cook chicken in heated large non-stick frying pan until browned both sides and almost cooked through. Add kecap manis to pan; cook until chicken is caramelised and cooked through. Remove chicken from pan, cover with foil; cool. Reserve any juices; slice chicken thickly.
Boil, steam or microwave asparagus until just tender; drain.
Cut carrot and snow peas into very thin strips. Combine asparagus, carrot, snow peas, sprouts, cabbage and onion in large bowl, top with chicken and reserved juices; drizzle with dressing. Sprinkle salad with nuts and seeds.
Dressing Combine ingredients in screw-top jar; shake well.

SERVES 4
Per serving
12.1g fat; 1253kJ

steamed **fish** cutlets
with ginger and soy

8 blue-eye
cutlets (800g)

2 teaspoons
sesame oil

2 tablespoons
light soy sauce

1 tablespoon mirin

1 clove garlic, crushed

2 x 4cm pieces fresh
ginger, sliced thinly

2 green onions,
sliced thinly

800g baby bok choy,
halved lengthways

Line a bamboo or metal steamer with baking paper. Place fish in steamer in single layer; drizzle with combined oil, soy, mirin and garlic. Top with ginger and onion. Cook fish, covered tightly, over wok or pan of simmering water about 5 minutes or until fish is just cooked through.
Meanwhile, stir-fry bok choy in heated oiled wok or large frying pan until just wilted. Serve fish with bok choy.

SERVES 4
Per serving 6.3g fat; 910kJ

500g seafood marinara mix

1 teaspoon olive oil

1 small red onion (100g), chopped finely

2 cloves garlic, crushed

2 x 400g cans tomatoes

1/2 cup (125ml) chicken stock

1/4 cup (60ml) dry white wine

2 tablespoons tomato paste

250g medium uncooked prawns, shelled

200g scallops

500g fettuccine

1 tablespoon finely shredded fresh basil

2 tablespoons finely chopped fresh flat-leaf parsley

Rinse marinara mix under cold water; drain well.
Heat oil in large saucepan; cook onion and garlic, stirring, until onion is soft. Add undrained crushed tomatoes, stock, wine and paste; simmer, uncovered, about 15 minutes or until sauce is thick.
Add seafood to sauce; simmer, uncovered, about 5 minutes or until seafood is just cooked through.
Meanwhile, cook pasta in large saucepan of boiling water, uncovered, until just tender; drain.
Stir basil and parsley into marinara sauce; serve over pasta.

SERVES 4
Per serving 7.3g fat; 2970kJ

oven-baked chicken schnitzels
with spicy wedges

1kg potatoes

1 egg white, beaten lightly

¼ teaspoon cayenne pepper

½ teaspoon sweet paprika

750g chicken thigh fillets

⅓ cup (50g) plain flour

2 egg whites, beaten lightly, extra

½ cup (50g) packaged breadcrumbs

½ cup (35g) corn flake crumbs

Preheat oven to hot. Cut unpeeled potatoes into wedges. Place potato, egg white, cayenne and paprika in large bowl; toss to combine. Place wedges, in single layer, skin-side down, in oiled shallow baking dish. Bake, uncovered, in hot oven 45 minutes or until browned and tender; keep warm.
Increase oven temperature to very hot. Using a meat mallet, flatten chicken to 5mm thickness. Toss chicken in flour, shake away excess. Dip chicken in extra egg white; toss in combined crumbs. Place chicken in single layer on oiled oven tray; bake, uncovered, in very hot oven about 15 minutes, turning halfway, until browned and cooked through.
Serve chicken and potato wedges with sweet chilli sauce and lime wedges, if desired.

SERVES 4
Per serving 14.5g fat; 2324kJ

spinach and pumpkin
curry

1kg pumpkin, peeled

1 tablespoon ghee

2 medium brown
onions (300g),
sliced thinly

2 cloves garlic,
crushed

1 teaspoon grated
fresh ginger

2 green thai chillies,
seeded, sliced thinly

1 teaspoon
ground coriander

1 teaspoon
ground cumin

1 teaspoon black
mustard seeds

1/2 teaspoon
ground turmeric

11/2 cups (375ml)
chicken stock

150g spinach,
chopped coarsely

1/3 cup loosely packed
fresh coriander

1 tablespoon flaked
almonds, toasted

Cut pumpkin into 3cm pieces.
Heat ghee in large saucepan; cook onion,
stirring, until browned. Add garlic, ginger,
chilli and spices; stir over heat until fragrant.
Add pumpkin and stock; simmer, covered,
about 15 minutes or until pumpkin is tender.
Add spinach and coriander; stir, tossing, until
spinach has just wilted.
Just before serving, sprinkle nuts over curry.

SERVES 4
Per serving 7.4g fat; 686kJ

thai-style
chicken skewers

750g chicken tenderloins

3 cloves garlic, crushed

2 teaspoons sugar

2 teaspoons
ground turmeric

2 teaspoons
sweet paprika

1 teaspoon mild
curry powder

1 tablespoon finely
chopped fresh coriander

2 tablespoons sweet
chilli sauce

2 tablespoons lime juice

1 lebanese cucumber
(130g), seeded,
sliced thinly

1 tablespoon unsalted
roasted peanuts,
chopped coarsely

chilli coriander sauce

2 tablespoons
rice vinegar

2 tablespoons sweet
chilli sauce

1 teaspoon finely
chopped fresh coriander

Cut tenderloins in half lengthways; thread chicken onto 12 skewers. Place skewers into large shallow dish; coat with combined garlic, sugar, spices, coriander, sauce and juice, cover; refrigerate at least 3 hours or until required.

Drain skewers from marinade; discard marinade. Cook skewers on heated oiled grill plate (or grill or barbecue) until browned all over and cooked through.

Serve skewers with chilli coriander sauce and cucumber; sprinkled with nuts.

Chilli Coriander Sauce
Combine ingredients in small bowl; mix well.

SERVES 4
Per serving 12.3g fat; 1279kJ

sichuan-style prawns
with rice noodles

40 medium uncooked
prawns (1kg)

2 tablespoons
sichuan peppercorns

4 star anise

1 teaspoon sea salt

420g fresh
rice noodles

1 tablespoon
peanut oil

400g baby bok choy,
chopped coarsely

500g choy sum,
chopped coarsely

1/3 cup (80ml)
oyster sauce

1 tablespoon light
soy sauce

Shell and devein prawns, leaving tails intact.
Crush peppercorns, star anise and salt; coat prawns in spice mixture.
Place noodles in large bowl, cover with warm water; gently
separate noodles with hands. Soak noodles 1 minute, drain;
rinse under cold water, drain.
Heat half of the oil in wok or large frying pan; stir-fry prawns, in batches,
until just changed in colour. Heat remaining oil in same pan; stir-fry
noodles, bok choy, choy sum and sauces, tossing, until noodles are hot
and vegetables are just wilted. Serve noodles topped with prawns.

SERVES 4
Per serving 2.7g fat; 1181kJ

lamb with caramelised
onions and potato salad

2 teaspoons
reduced-fat
margarine

2 medium red
onions (340g),
sliced thinly

1/3 cup (80ml)
raspberry vinegar

1 tablespoon
brown sugar

1/4 cup (60ml)
water

350g lamb
backstraps

potato salad

400g baby new
potatoes, halved

500g asparagus,
trimmed

350g watercress

1 tablespoon dijon
mustard

2 cloves garlic,
crushed

1 tablespoon
lemon juice

Melt margarine in large non-stick frying pan;
cook onion, stirring, until soft. Add vinegar, sugar
and the water; cook, stirring, until sugar dissolves.
Simmer, uncovered, stirring occasionally, about
10 minutes or until onion is caramelised.

Meanwhile, cook lamb on heated oiled grill plate
(or grill or barbecue) until browned all over and
cooked as desired; stand, covered, 5 minutes
before slicing. Serve with caramelised onions
and potato salad.

Potato Salad Boil, steam or microwave potato and
asparagus, separately, until tender. Combine potato,
asparagus and watercress in large bowl, add
combined remaining ingredients; toss gently.

SERVES 4
Per serving 4.9g fat; 1055kJ

salmon and dill
tortellini salad

375g spinach and ricotta tortellini

¹/₂ cup (140g) low-fat yogurt

2 teaspoons seeded mustard

¹/₄ cup (60ml) oil-free italian dressing

2 teaspoons finely chopped fresh dill

2 tablespoons water

1 teaspoon sugar

415g can red salmon, drained

1 tablespoon drained capers

2 sticks trimmed celery (150g), sliced thinly

1 lebanese cucumber (130g), sliced thinly

Cook pasta in large saucepan of boiling water, uncovered, until just tender; drain. Rinse pasta under cold water; cool.

Meanwhile, combine yogurt, mustard, dressing, dill, the water and sugar in small bowl; whisk until dressing is smooth.

Combine pasta with flaked salmon, capers, celery and cucumber in large bowl. Just before serving, drizzle with dressing.

SERVES 4
Per serving 10.1g fat; 953kJ

roasted eggplant with
capsicum and pesto

1 large red
capsicum (350g)

14 baby eggplants
(840g)

coarse cooking salt

4 slices wholemeal
bread

2 tablespoons flaked
parmesan cheese

marinade

1/3 cup (80ml)
lemon juice

1 tablespoon
balsamic vinegar

3 teaspoons sweet
chilli sauce

2 teaspoons sugar

2 cloves garlic,
crushed

2 teaspoons
olive oil

pesto

1 1/2 cups loosely
packed fresh basil

2 tablespoons
fresh oregano

2/3 cup (130g) low-
fat ricotta cheese

2 tablespoons water

Quarter capsicum, remove and discard seeds and membranes. Roast under grill or in very hot oven, skin-side up, until skin blisters and blackens. Cover capsicum with plastic or paper for 5 minutes, peel away skin and discard. Slice capsicum thinly.
Cut eggplants into four slices lengthways; place in colander, sprinkle with salt, stand 30 minutes. Rinse slices; drain on absorbent paper. Combine eggplant and marinade in bowl, cover; refrigerate 30 minutes.
Drain eggplant, reserve marinade. Grill eggplant, brushing with reserved marinade, until browned and tender. Remove crusts, then toast bread; top toast with eggplant, capsicum, cheese and pesto.
Marinade Combine ingredients in small bowl.
Pesto Blend or process ingredients with 1/4 cup (60ml) of reserved marinade until smooth.

SERVES 4
Per serving 7.4g fat; 535kJ

italian-style
chicken with
tomatoes and oregano

4 chicken thigh cutlets (640g), skin removed

1 large brown onion (200g), chopped finely

2 cloves garlic, crushed

1/2 cup (125ml) chicken stock

2 x 400g cans tomatoes

2 tablespoons tomato paste

1 teaspoon sugar

2 tablespoons red wine vinegar

500g button mushrooms

2 teaspoons finely chopped fresh oregano

8 small zucchini (720g), halved lengthways

cooking-oil spray

Cook chicken in oiled large saucepan until browned both sides, remove chicken from pan.

Cook onion, garlic and stock in same pan, uncovered, about 5 minutes or until onion softens and liquid has evaporated. Return chicken to pan with undrained crushed tomatoes, paste, sugar, vinegar, mushrooms and oregano; simmer, covered, 1 hour. Remove lid; simmer about 15 minutes or until chicken is tender and sauce has thickened slightly.

Meanwhile, coat zucchini with cooking-oil spray; cook on heated oiled grill plate (or grill or barbecue) until browned both sides and tender.

Serve chicken mixture with char-grilled zucchini; season with freshly ground black pepper and top with fresh oregano leaves, if desired.

SERVES 4
Per serving 10.4g fat; 1197kJ

peppered
pork curry

¾ cup (210g)
low-fat yogurt

1 tablespoon cracked
black pepper

2 tablespoons grated
fresh ginger

4 cloves garlic,
crushed

2 tablespoons
lemon juice

2 teaspoons
garam masala

1 teaspoon
ground coriander

1 teaspoon
ground turmeric

500g pork fillet,
sliced thickly

400g can tomatoes

1 teaspoon sugar

¾ cup (180ml)
chicken stock

350g green beans

500g butternut
pumpkin, chopped
coarsely

¼ cup coarsely
chopped fresh
coriander

Combine yogurt, pepper, ginger, garlic, juice,
spices and pork in large bowl, cover; refrigerate
at least 3 hours or until required.

Heat a large non-stick saucepan; cook pork
mixture, in batches, until pork is browned
lightly. Return pork to pan with undrained
crushed tomatoes, sugar, stock and beans;
simmer, covered, about 15 minutes or until
pork is tender.

Meanwhile, boil, steam or microwave
pumpkin until tender; drain. Add pumpkin
and coriander to curry just before serving.

SERVES 4
Per serving 5.1g fat; 1136kJ

ricotta

and spinach pasta shells

*32 large pasta
shells (280g)*

500g spinach

*1¼ cups (250g)
low-fat ricotta cheese*

*2½ cups (500g)
low-fat cottage cheese*

*1½ cups (375ml)
tomato pasta sauce*

*1 cup (250ml)
vegetable stock*

*1 tablespoon
finely grated
parmesan cheese*

Cook pasta in large saucepan of boiling water, uncovered, 3 minutes;
drain, cool slightly.
Preheat oven to moderate. Boil, steam or microwave spinach until just
wilted; drain. Squeeze excess moisture from spinach; chop spinach
finely. Combine ricotta and cottage cheese with spinach in medium bowl.
Spoon the spinach mixture into pasta shells.
Combine sauce and stock in shallow 2-litre (8 cup) ovenproof dish;
arrange pasta shells in the sauce mixture, sprinkle with parmesan.
Bake, covered, in moderate oven about 1 hour or until pasta is tender.

SERVES 4
Per serving 13.2g fat; 2415kJ

honey and soy
roast pork

2 large pork
fillets (750g)

750g kumara,
sliced thickly

1 tablespoon
seeded mustard

2 tablespoons honey

1 tablespoon light
soy sauce

4 green onions,
sliced thinly

Preheat oven to very hot. Cut each pork fillet in
half. Place the pork and kumara in oiled baking
dish. Pour over the combined mustard, honey
and sauce; toss to coat pork and kumara in the
honey mixture. Bake, uncovered, in very hot
oven, about 25 minutes or until pork and
kumara are browned and cooked through.
Slice pork; serve with kumara, topped with
green onions. Serve with steamed beans
and snow peas, if desired.

SERVES 4
Per serving 4.6g fat; 1509kJ

warm lamb salad with
yogurt mint dressing

150g dry-packed
sun-dried tomatoes

400g lamb fillets

1 medium yellow
capsicum (200g)

1 red oakleaf lettuce

1 small red onion (100g),
sliced thinly

yogurt mint dressing

3/4 cup (210g)
low-fat yogurt

2 tablespoons coarsely
chopped fresh mint

1/4 teaspoon
ground cumin

2 teaspoons lemon juice

Place tomatoes in medium heatproof bowl, cover with boiling water; stand about 5 minutes or until soft. Drain tomatoes; cut in half.

Cook lamb on heated oiled grill plate (or grill or barbecue) until browned all over and cooked as desired. Cover, rest lamb 5 minutes; slice thinly.

Quarter capsicum; remove seeds and membranes, discard. Roast under grill or in very hot oven, skin-side up, until skin blisters and blackens. Cover capsicum with plastic or paper for 5 minutes, peel away skin and discard.

Combine lettuce leaves, onion, thinly sliced capsicum, tomato and lamb in large bowl; drizzle with yogurt mint dressing.

Yogurt Mint Dressing Whisk ingredients in small bowl until combined.

SERVES 4
Per serving 6.4g fat; 1083kJ

54 beef steaks with
roasted capsicums

4 small beef fillet steaks (600g)

2 tablespoons seeded mustard

1 tablespoon worcestershire sauce

1 tablespoon balsamic vinegar

2 cloves garlic, crushed

roasted capsicums

2 medium red capsicums (400g)

1 medium yellow capsicum (200g)

1 medium green capsicum (200g)

1 teaspoon olive oil

1 tablespoon balsamic vinegar

1/2 teaspoon dried crushed chillies

1 clove garlic, crushed

1 tablespoon finely chopped fresh flat-leaf parsley

1 teaspoon finely chopped fresh thyme

Combine beef with mustard, sauce, vinegar and garlic in large bowl, cover; refrigerate at least 3 hours or until required. Drain steaks over small bowl; discard marinade.
Cook steaks on heated oiled grill plate (or grill or barbecue) until browned both sides and cooked as desired. Add roasted capsicums to grill plate; cook until hot. Serve steaks with roasted capsicums.
Roasted Capsicums Quarter capsicums, remove and discard seeds and membranes. Roast under grill or in very hot oven, skin-side up, until skin blisters and blackens. Cover capsicum pieces with plastic or paper for 5 minutes, peel away skin and discard. Combine hot capsicum in medium bowl with oil, vinegar, chilli, garlic and herbs.

SERVES 4
Per serving 8.9g fat; 1047kJ

veal with garlic mushrooms
and asparagus

4 veal steaks (600g)

350g small cup
mushrooms

¾ cup (180ml)
chicken stock

2 cloves garlic,
crushed

300g asparagus,
chopped coarsely

1 teaspoon cornflour

2 teaspoons water

2 tablespoons flaked
parmesan cheese

Cook veal, in batches, in heated oiled large
non-stick frying pan, until browned both sides.
Remove veal from pan, cover to keep warm.
Cook mushrooms, stock and garlic in same pan,
covered, about 5 minutes or until mushrooms
soften. Add asparagus; cook, covered, until
asparagus is just tender. Stir in blended
cornflour and water; stir until sauce boils
and thickens. Serve veal with mushroom
mixture; top with cheese.

SERVES 4
Per serving 5.2g fat; 884kJ

seasoned beef
fillet

1 medium brown onion (150g), chopped finely

2 tablespoons finely chopped walnuts

$1/2$ cup (35g) stale breadcrumbs

$1/2$ teaspoon finely grated orange rind

1 tablespoon dry red wine

$1/4$ cup (70g) seeded mustard

2 tablespoons finely chopped fresh chives

500g piece beef fillet

$1/2$ cup (125ml) orange juice

Heat oiled small saucepan; cook onion, stirring, until soft. Combine onion, nuts, breadcrumbs, rind, wine, 2 tablespoons of the mustard and chives in small bowl.

Preheat oven to hot. Cut deep pocket in side of beef, place seasoning in pocket; secure with kitchen string. Heat oiled flameproof baking dish; brown beef all over. Roast beef, uncovered, in hot oven about 25 minutes or until cooked as desired. Remove beef from dish, cover, rest 5 minutes; slice thickly.

Heat same dish, stir in remaining mustard and juice; cook, stirring, until mixture boils. Serve sauce with beef.

SERVES 4
Per serving 11.4g fat; 1125kJ

chicken with sautéed tomatoes, basil and fetta

500g chicken tenderloins

1 teaspoon cajun seasoning

2 medium red onions (340g)

2 cloves garlic, crushed

1/2 cup (125ml) chicken stock

2 tablespoons balsamic vinegar

500g cherry tomatoes

100g low-fat fetta cheese, crumbled

2 tablespoons finely shredded fresh basil

Combine chicken and seasoning in medium bowl; mix well. Cut onions into thin wedges.

Cook chicken in heated large non-stick frying pan until browned all over and cooked through; remove from pan, keep warm.

Cook onion, garlic and stock in same pan, covered, about 10 minutes or until onion is very soft. Remove lid; simmer until liquid has evaporated. Add vinegar; cook, stirring, until onion is caramelised. Add tomatoes; cook until just softened.

Slice chicken; serve topped with sautéed tomatoes, cheese and basil.

SERVES 4
Per serving 10.9g fat; 1162kJ

glossary

bacon rashers also known as slices of bacon; made from cured, smoked pork side.

bok choy also known as pak choi or chinese white cabbage; mildly mustard-tasting green vegetable. Stems and leaves are used. Baby bok choy is also available.

borlotti beans pale brown beans with burgundy-coloured markings.

breadcrumbs

packaged: fine-textured, crunchy, commercially purchased breadcrumbs.

stale: one- or two-day-old bread made into crumbs by grating, blending or processing.

butter beans also known as cannellini beans; small white beans.

cajun seasoning packaged blend of assorted herbs and spices that can include paprika, basil, onion, fennel, thyme, cayenne and tarragon.

capers the grey-green buds of a warm-climate shrub; capers are sold either dried and salted, or pickled in a vinegar brine.

capsicum also known as bell pepper or, simply, pepper.

chicken, tenderloins thin strip of meat lying just under the breast.

chilli, thai red to dark-green in colour, they are small, medium-to-hot chillies.

choy sum also known as flowering bok choy or flowering white cabbage.

cornflour also known as cornstarch; used as a thickening agent.

couscous a fine, grain-like cereal product; made from semolina.

eggplant also known as aubergine.

fish sauce also called nam pla or nuoc nam; made from pulverised salted fermented fish. Has pungent smell and strong taste.

flour, plain all-purpose flour, made from wheat.

garam masala a blend of spices, including cardamom, cinnamon, clove, coriander, fennel and cumin, roasted and ground together.

ghee clarified butter; with the milk solids removed, it can be heated to a high temperature without burning.

golden syrup a by-product of refined sugarcane; pure maple syrup or honey can be substituted.

hoisin sauce a thick, sweet and spicy Chinese paste made from salted fermented soy beans, onions and garlic.

kecap manis Indonesian thick soy sauce which has sugar and spices added.

kumara Polynesian name of orange-fleshed sweet potato often confused with yam.

lamb

backstrap: the larger fillet from a row of loin chops or cutlets.

eye of loin: a cut derived from a row of loin chops; once the bone and fat are removed, the larger portion is known as the eye of loin.

lemon grass a tall, clumping, lemon-smelling and -tasting, sharp-edged grass; the white lower part of the stem is used in cooking.

mesclun a salad mix with a mixture of assorted young lettuce and other green leaves, including baby spinach leaves, mizuna, curly endive, etc.

milk, skim we used milk with 0.1% fat content.

mirin sweet low-alcohol rice wine used in Japanese cooking.

mushrooms, straw cultivated Chinese mushroom; sold canned in brine.

noodles

bean thread vermicelli: also known as bean thread noodles, or cellophane or glass noodles.

fresh rice: thick, wide, almost white in colour; made from rice and vegetable oil. Cover with boiling water to remove starch and excess oil before using.

oil

peanut: oil pressed from ground peanuts; has high smoke point.

sesame: oil made from roasted sesame seeds; a flavouring rather than a cooking medium.

onion

green: also known as scallion or (incorrectly) shallot; an immature onion picked before bulb forms. Has long, green edible stalk.

red: also known as Spanish, red Spanish or Bermuda onion; large, sweet-flavoured, purple-red onion.

oyster sauce made from oyster extract, sugars, salt and other flavourings.

prawns also known as shrimp.

pumpkin also known as squash.

rice vinegar made from fermented rice, colourless and flavoured with sugar and salt. Also known as seasoned rice vinegar.

scallops a bivalve mollusc with fluted shell.

seafood marinara mix a commercial mixture of raw chopped seafood.

sichuan pepper (also known as szechuan or chinese pepper) small, red-brown aromatic seeds; they have a peppery-lemon flavour.

snake beans long (about 40cm), thin, round green beans, Asian in origin.

snow peas also called mange tout ("eat all").

spinach leafy vegetable often incorrectly called silverbeet. A "baby" variety is also available.

star anise dried star-shaped pod; has an aniseed flavour.

sugar we used coarse granulated table sugar (crystal sugar) unless otherwise specified.

brown: a soft, fine sugar retaining molasses.

tamarind concentrate thick, dark, ready-to-use paste; extract of tamarind bean.

tofu also known as bean curd, an off-white, custard-like product made from the "milk" of crushed soy beans.

tomato, paste triple-concentrated tomato puree.

wasabi an Asian horseradish used to make a fiery sauce traditionally served with Japanese raw fish dishes.

watercress small, crisp, deep-green rounded leaves with a slightly bitter, peppery flavour.

zucchini also known as courgette.

index

facts and figures

These conversions are approximate only, but the difference between an exact and the approximate conversion of various liquid and dry measures is minimal and will not affect your cooking results.

Note: NZ, Canada, USA and UK all use 15ml tablespoons. Australian tablespoons measure 20ml.
All cup and spoon measurements are level.

Measuring equipment

The difference between one country's measuring cups and another's is, at most, within a 2 or 3 teaspoon variance. (For the record, 1 Australian metric measuring cup holds approximately 250ml.) The most accurate way of measuring dry ingredients is to weigh them. For liquids, use a clear glass or plastic jug having metric markings.

How to measure

When using graduated measuring cups, shake dry ingredients loosely into the appropriate cup. Do not tap the cup on a bench or tightly pack the ingredients unless directed to do so. Level the top of measuring cups and measuring spoons with a knife. When measuring liquids, place a clear glass or plastic jug having metric markings on a flat surface to check accuracy at eye level.

Dry Measures

metric	imperial
15g	1/2oz
30g	1oz
60g	2oz
90g	3oz
125g	4oz (1/4lb)
155g	5oz
185g	6oz
220g	7oz
250g	8oz (1/2lb)
280g	9oz
315g	10oz
345g	11oz
375g	12oz (3/4lb)
410g	13oz
440g	14oz
470g	15oz
500g	16oz (1lb)
750g	24oz (1 1/2lb)
1kg	32oz (2lb)

We use large eggs having an average weight of 60g.

Liquid Measures

metric	imperial
30ml	1 fluid oz
60ml	2 fluid oz
100ml	3 fluid oz
125ml	4 fluid oz
150ml	5 fluid oz (1/4 pint/1 gill)
190ml	6 fluid oz
250ml (1cup)	8 fluid oz
300ml	10 fluid oz (1/2 pint)
500ml	16 fluid oz
600ml	20 fluid oz (1 pint)
1000ml (1litre)	1 3/4 pints

Helpful Measures

metric	imperial
3mm	1/8in
6mm	1/4in
1cm	1/2in
2cm	3/4in
2.5cm	1in
6cm	2 1/2in
8cm	3in
20cm	8in
23cm	9in
25cm	10in
30cm	12in (1ft)

Oven Temperatures

These oven temperatures are only a guide.
Always check the manufacturer's manual.

	°C (Celsius)	°F (Fahrenheit)	Gas Mark
Very slow	120	250	1
Slow	150	300	2
Moderately slow	160	325	3
Moderate	180–190	350–375	4
Moderately hot	200–210	400–425	5
Hot	220–230	450–475	6
Very hot	240–250	500–525	7

at your fingertips

These elegant slipcovers store up to 10 mini books and make the books instantly accessible.

And the metric measuring cups and spoons make following our recipes a piece of cake.

Book Holder
Australia and overseas:
$A8.95 (incl. GST).

Metric Measuring Set
Australia: $6.50 (incl. GST).
New Zealand: $A8.00.
Elsewhere: $A9.95.
Prices include postage
and handling.
This offer is available
in all countries.

Photocopy and complete the coupon below

Mail or fax Photocopy and complete the coupon below and post to AWW Home Library Reader Offer, ACP Direct, PO Box 7036, Sydney NSW 1028, *or* fax to (02) 9267 4363.

Phone Have your credit card details ready, then, if you live in Sydney, phone 9260 0000; if you live elsewhere in Australia, phone 1800 252 515 (free call, Mon-Fri, 8.30am - 5.30pm).

Australian residents We accept the credit cards listed on the coupon, money orders and cheques.

Overseas residents We accept the credit cards listed on the coupon, drafts in $A drawn on an Australian bank, and also British, New Zealand and U.S. cheques in the currency of the country of issue.

Food editor Pamela Clark
Associate food editor Karen Hammial
Assistant food editor Kathy McGarry
Assistant recipe editor Elizabeth Hooper

HOME LIBRARY STAFF
Editor-in-chief Susan Tomnay
Editor Julie Collard
Concept design Jackie Richards
Designer Caryl Wiggins
Book sales manager Jennifer McDonald
Production manager Carol Currie

Publisher Sue Wannan
Group publisher Jill Baker
Chief executive officer John Alexander

Produced by *The Australian Women's Weekly* Home Library, Sydney.

Colour separations by
ACP Colour Graphics Pty Ltd, Sydney.
Printing by Dai Nippon Printing in Hong Kong.

Published by ACP Publishing Pty Limited,
54 Park St, Sydney; GPO Box 4088, Sydney,
NSW 1028. Ph: (02) 9282 8618
Fax: (02) 9267 9438.

awwhomelib@acp.com.au
www.awwbooks.com.au

Australia Distributed by Network Distribution Company, GPO Box 4088, Sydney, NSW 102
Ph: (02) 9282 8777 Fax: (02) 9264 3278.

United Kingdom Distributed by Australian Consolidated Press (UK), Moulton Park Business Centre, Red House Road, Moulton Park, Northampton, NN3 6AQ. Ph: (01604) 497 53
Fax: (01604) 497 533 acpukltd@aol.com

Canada Distributed by Whitecap Books Ltd, 351 Lynn Ave, North Vancouver, BC, V7J 2C4
Ph: (604) 980 9852.

New Zealand Distributed by Netlink Distribut Company, Level 4, 23 Hargreaves St, College Hill, Auckland 1, Ph: (9) 302 7616.

South Africa Distributed by:
PSD Promotions (Pty) Ltd, PO Box 1175, Isando 1600, SA, Ph: (011) 392 6065; and CNA Limited, Newsstand Division, PO Box 1
Johannesburg 2000. Ph: (011) 491 7500.

Light and Lean.

Includes index.
ISBN 1 86396 244 1

1. Low-fat cookery – recipes.
I. Title: Australian Women's Weekly.
(Series: Australian Women's Weekly
Healthy Eating mini series)

641.5638

© ACP Publishing Pty Limited 2001
ABN 18 053 273 546

This publication is copyright. No part of it may be reproduced or transmitted in any form without written permission of the publishers.

Cover: Swordfish with beans and tomatoes, page 14.
Photographer: Alan Benson
Back cover: Asian-style chicken salad, page

The publishers would like to thank Mud Australia for props used in photography.